MW01287083

Autism

Understanding the Puzzle

By Sharla R. Jordan

Illustrations by Amy L. Seiter

Lulu Publishing

Raleigh, North Carolina

ISBN 978-1-105-02933-2

Printed in the United States of America

Helping a child who has autism requires personal dedication, quality professional services, and unwavering support from loved ones. For me, my greatest support comes from my dear husband, who sustains all my efforts and who loves our boys and me unconditionally.

I thank the many people who helped and inspired me to write this book: my husband, family, friends, medical professionals, parents of children with autism, and especially my boys; they are my heroes. This book is dedicated to my boys.

The puzzle piece is the symbol for autism.
It was developed in 1963
by the National Autistic Society.

About the Author

Sharla R. Jordan was born and raised in Mesa, Arizona, ninth in a family of ten children. She graduated from Mountain View High School and Mesa Community College, with two associate degrees. She is currently enrolled at Weber State University in Ogden, Utah with a major in psychology and a minor in music.

She resides in Kaysville, Utah with her husband and their six sons, four of whom are on the autism spectrum. Sharla loves her family, music, learning, and sharing her knowledge and experiences with others. She is passionate about helping her boys and others who work with those challenged by autism. This has motivated her to write this concise and easy to read book.

About the Illustrator

Amy L. Seiter was born and raised in Mesa, Arizona. At an early age, Amy showed a natural talent for drawing as a preschooler, she did her first collaborative work: illustrating stories written by her older sister. Today, Amy's artistic talent extends into several mediums, but her preference is pencil drawings.

Known for her love of all children, Amy is blessed with a natural ability for understanding and interacting with those who are often misunderstood. She expresses her sincere appreciation to those who love and care for children with autism throughout the world.

Table of Contents

What Simple Techniques Can I Use to Help Calm or Soothe a

Child with Autism?..... 38

Introduction

This book gives you clear and simple explanations of autism spectrum disorder. Whether you are new to autism or have had years of experience in helping someone with autism, it will help you better understand autism's puzzle.

Throughout the world, parents of children with autism want those closest to them to understand how autism affects their children and families. Parents frequently have difficulty explaining to others what is going on with their children and all that the disorder entails. In addition, much emotion, energy, and time is required to nurture a child with autism. Often, parents are tired and don't have much energy left over to explain what is happening in their lives.

As the mother of six boys, four of whom are on the autism spectrum, I wanted to understand autism—what it was and how to help my sons. However, I could not find a book that would explain things in a simple way or that was short enough that I felt I had time to read it. I was already overwhelmed with the demands of my sons' challenges, and I didn't have time to read a lengthy, complicated book or do extensive research on the Internet.

This is the book I wish I'd had when my boys were first diagnosed—the handbook I wanted when I needed a quick question answered. It is the resource I wished I'd had to share with my family and friends when they were trying to understand or help.

Here, I share information that has helped our family and given us hope through hard times. I also touch on a few of my personal experiences and share insightful comments from other parents.

Autism: Understanding the Puzzle does not address every aspect of autism and its complexities. It covers general information and provides resources for further study.

Chapter 1

Answers to Your Basic Questions

What Is Autism?
It's a Complex Brain Disorder

"Autism is the general term used to describe a group of complex developmental brain disorders known as pervasive developmental disorder (PDD)" *(Autism Speaks)*. Parents and professionals refer to it as autism or autism spectrum disorder (ASD). With autism, the brain functions differently than a neuro-typical (normal) brain. Autism affects the way someone perceives the world and how he or she functions in it. Autism affects a person's developmental abilities in communication, social skills and behaviors, and often his or her education, health, and nutrition. *(Autism Speaks)*

Additional physical and mental health issues may accompany autism spectrum disorder. These issues may include Tourette syndrome, seizures, and gastro-intestinal problems; a very high percentage of individuals with autism also have depression and/or anxiety.

Why Is It Called a Spectrum Disorder?

Autism is like an umbrella. It is made up of five sub-groups that are specific to their degree of developmental strengths and challenges.

- **Autistic Disorder**
- **Asperger Syndrome**
- **Pervasive Developmental Disorder—Not Otherwise Specified (PDD-NOS)**

- **Rett Syndrome**
- **Childhood Disintegrative Disorder**

What Causes Autism?

No one knows the exact cause of autism. Scientists believe that there isn't just one cause. We do know there are multiple genetic and environmental factors.

During clinical visits with our psychiatrist, we learned that a child is at high risk for autism if there is depression in both the mother's and father's families. Also, if a couple has identical twins, and one has an autism spectrum disorder, the other has a 90 percent chance of having ASD as well.

The high genetic component isn't the sole cause. Environmental factors (that have yet to be identified) contribute to autism as well. A very high percentage of individuals with autism experienced a traumatic event or health condition during their pre-, peri-, or postnatal periods of life. A large amount of research is currently being conducted to discover some of the possible causes and the links between genetics and environment factors.

Autism spectrum disorders can begin as early as birth or during early childhood. The onset may be sudden after typical development. Severe autism is usually diagnosed earlier because larger differences in children's developmental delays can be easily recognized. Moderate to mild autism is usually diagnosed after children are three years old and by the time they are eight. However, autism can be diagnosed in adults as well.

Autism Is Not Caused By Bad Parenting!!!

Sixty years ago, doctors believed autism was caused by bad parenting. Research and awareness of the disorder has changed that once devastating conclusion, and this understanding has relieved the burden of guilt that many parents felt when they believed that they caused their child's autism disorder. Autism is never the fault of the child or the parents.

Autism doesn't just go away.
They may make improvements,
but it is still a lifelong challenge.

– Shannon

Are There Cures for Autism Spectrum Disorders?

Not yet. ASDs are considered lifelong. However, physicians and researchers believe that over time, with many therapies and services, the symptoms can be minimized and quality of life can improve. Some people with autism have had their diagnoses changed because of significant improvements, but this is very rare and individuals usually retain some social and language delays. The earlier a child is diagnosed and receives therapy and services, and the earlier parents receive support and educate themselves about the disorder, the better the child's developmental outcome will be.

How Common Is Autism?

Autism is very common. According to the most current statistics taken in 2006, from the Center for Disease Control and Prevention (CDC) and the Autism and Developmental Disabilities Monitoring (ADDM) Network, **one in every 110 children in the United States has an ASD. One in every 70 is a boy**. The ratio of boys to girls is four to one. (*Center for Disease Control and Prevention's and Autism and Developmental Disabilities Monitoring*) Recent studies have discovered that **younger siblings of those with autism have a 19% higher risk** for developing autism (Tanner).

Autism can affect anyone—regardless of race, ethnicity, or background. It is more common than childhood cancer, juvenile diabetes and pediatric AIDS combined. "An estimated 1.5 million individuals in the U.S. and tens of millions worldwide are affected by autism. Government statistics suggest that the prevalence rate of autism is increasing 10–17% annually" (*Autism Speaks*). In Utah this growth rate appears to be more aggressive: From 2002 to 2008, autism diagnoses have doubled in just six years. According to the latest study done in 2011, 1 in 77 eight year olds in Utah have an ASD. In 2008, the daily average of babies born was 150. Thus, on average, **two babies born every day in Utah will be diagnosed with an ASD.** (Leonard)

Multiple factors account for these increased numbers. Improvement in diagnostic methods is one factor in the escalation in diagnoses. In the 1980s and 90s, the Diagnostic and Statistical Manuel of Mental Disorders (DSM III) had a much narrower range of classification for autism. In 1994, the DSM IV made changes to include those people whose symptoms were not as severe. In addition, public awareness has helped parents to be less afraid of judgment and labels as they were in the past, thus motivating them to seek professional help.

Undiagnosed individuals have been around for centuries. Very likely, you knew individuals during your school years that may have had a mild form of autism. They might have been socially awkward or preferred to be alone. They may have had superior intelligence but were slow to respond. To you, their behavior seemed to be "off" or strange. Perhaps they spoke in a loud or monotone voice. They may have had their own style or fashion, much like the character Steve Urkel in the TV show *Family Matters*. Today, you may know a 40-year-old man who is extremely intelligent, has four college degrees, but is unable to keep a job and still lives at home with his parents.

In years past, the majority of individuals with moderate to severe autism either stayed at home or were placed in an institution. Parents did not have the resources or choices that are available today to help them to care for their child. People with milder forms of autism struggled to find a place where they could "fit" or succeed in this world; many are still trying to find that place.

Thankfully, through new research and by listening to those who have autism, professionals have gained a greater understanding of autism. This understanding has helped them know what treatment options to implement to improve the developmental abilities of those with an ASD.

Even though wonderful treatment options are now available, a large number of children still are not receiving services. One reason for this is supply: We don't have enough qualified respite providers, special education teachers, therapists, doctors, and specialists. There are also insufficient resources available to meet the growing number of individuals on the autism spectrum. There is also a shortage of services for adults, and the need is only going to grow as the estimated 800,000 eight year olds with ASDs in the United States mature into adulthood over the next ten years. To compound the problem, most insurance companies deny coverage for autism services and treatments for both adults and children.

How Is Autism Diagnosed?

Only a professional, such as a psychiatrist, psychologist, neurologist, or a developmental pediatrician can diagnosis a child with autism. There is not a simple test. **Diagnosis is based on a review of the child's developmental history, careful observations of his behaviors, and educational and psychological tests.** A team of specialists may do the evaluation, such as in public schools where a school psychologist, occupational therapist, speech therapist, audiologist, and resource teacher would all take part.

An evaluation involves a large amount of paperwork for the parent, usually the mother, to fill out. Sometimes a teacher or childcare provider will fill out evaluation forms as well if they have spent large amounts of time with the child. These are used to help the professional determine the diagnosis. The test used will depend on the age of the child. Some, but not all, of the tests used to evaluate a child may include:

- Autistic Diagnostic Observation Schedule (ADOS)
- Autistic Diagnostic Interview (ADI)
- Childhood Autism Spectrum Test (CAST)
- Modified Checklist of Autism in Toddlers (MCHAT)

All evaluation tests must use the most current *Diagnostic Statistical Manuel of Mental Health* (DSM), to determine the criteria for a diagnosis. The most recent manual is the fourth edition (DSM IV), published in 1994. Online, you can read the DSM IV classifications for an ASD. I have provided the Website address and information in "Additional Information and Resources" at the end of this book in the "Online" section under the heading "DSM Diagnostic Criteria."

A new manual, DSM V, is being written and will include changes to the classifications of ASD. The proposed changes will eliminate the subgroup names. All subgroups will be placed under the diagnosis of autism spectrum disorder and then given a classification of type one or two, depending on the severity of symptoms. DSM V is scheduled to be published in 2012 or 2013. (American Psychiatric Association)

The symptoms for mental health issues can be very similar. Thus, a child may be misdiagnosed with another mental illness, developmental delay, or a learning disability before a correct diagnosis is given. One of our sons was diagnosed with attention deficit hyperactive disorder (ADHD) with depression and anxiety before he was correctly diagnosed years later with mild autism. It's a good idea to have more than one professional evaluate your child. If you suspect your child has autistic symptoms and your concerns are not validated, don't give up. Speak with multiple professionals. The younger the child is diagnosed, the better chance he has for improvement and success in his adult years. It is unfortunate when a child's diagnosis is delayed and he is left to battle his challenges without the benefits of therapy or services.

As a parent you can monitor your child from birth to three years of age. Ask yourself: How normal was the pregnancy and delivery? Were there any complications? Did the child achieve his developmental milestones on time, such as crawling, walking, talking, etc.? Many pediatricians screen children between the ages of 18–24 months during children's well-child visits. If your physician does not do this, ask him to do so. If autism is suspected, your pediatrician should refer you to someone who can do a complete evaluation. In addition, vision and hearing tests should be done to rule out other possible challenges.

A child with autism might not show delays in all areas. The opposite is also the case; a child could have a level of vocabulary much older than his years and still have autism. In addition, a child can have speech or other delays without having autism.

Be aware that sometimes signs of autism are not as noticeable in the early years, and you might not see symptoms until your child is older. Typically the more severe the symptoms are, the earlier you will notice the signs.

Could My Child Have Autism and I Don't See It?

Absolutely! Observing other children the same age can be helpful in recognizing what is normal and what is not. You may want to ask outside sources if they have noticed anything different from the norm in your child. It took several kind hints and gentle recommendations from teachers, family, friends, and professionals before I noticed my sons' symptoms and had my boys evaluated. I hadn't experienced a "normal" (neuro-typical) child until my third boy came along. It wasn't until then that I began thinking that something was off with the first two, but I didn't know what it was. How was I to know any differently? What I'd thought was "normal" development was actually autism. I'd figured "This is the terrible two's," even though my son was 12 years old. Or when my sons did something disruptive or unusual, I'd write it off, thinking "It's just a phase," or "They're just boys."

My son appears normal,
but if you spend
a fair amount of time with him
you will begin to see
that something is different.

Following is a list by *Autism Speaks.* These symptoms are not absolutes used to determine if a child has autism, but are "red flags" indicating a possibility of autism.

- No big smiles or other warm, joyful expressions by six months or thereafter
- No back-and-forth sharing of sounds, smiles, or other facial expressions by nine months or thereafter
- No babbling by 12 months
- No back-and-forth gestures, such as pointing, showing, reaching, or waving by 12 months
- No words by 16 months
- No two-word meaningful phrases (without imitating or repeating) by 24 months
- Any loss of speech or the ability to babble at any age
- Any loss of social skills at any age

The developmental milestones that a child should be reaching are found on the *Autism Speaks* Website.

What Should I Do
after My Child Is Diagnosed?

Begin to accept it. It is hard to process all the thoughts and emotions you feel after your child is diagnosed. It's overwhelming.

The acceptance process after a diagnosis is much like going through the stages of grief: denial, guilt, anger, blaming, bargaining, depression, and finally acceptance. You have suffered a loss. You have lost the dream of who you thought your child would be.

Accepting what autism meant for our boys took a lot of time. Even now, whenever new challenges arise, I cycle through the grieving process and its emotions again and again. I find comfort in writing down our journey in my journal. Writing helps me see where my boys began and the progress they are making now. Once I had accepted my boys' diagnoses and gotten all the self blame out of the way, I was able to search for help and find services and therapy that would benefit them and improve their development.

If you are a parent whose child has recently received a diagnosis and you want a packet of information to help you with the critical time following, I suggest going to the Website, *Autism Speaks*. There you will find a tool kit to help you week by week with the first 100 days.

When your child is first diagnosed, you might think that he will be just like another child you know who has autism. However, time will show that no two children and no two cases of autism are exactly alike. When you feel tempted to worry that your child will have the same severe challenges as does another child with autism, take comfort in knowing that each child is different. While many of the symptoms in each individual are similar, the number and degree of challenges are unique to each, in the same way that each human being has unique personalities, strengths, and weaknesses. My son, who has PDD-NOS, does not have the same degree of challenges as does his brother who has autism. They both have similar autistic symptoms, but they do not have the same challenges to overcome.

Remember your child is
still the same amazing and lovable self
as she was before she was diagnosed.
Autism is not who she is;
it is merely a descriptive word
that explains her unique qualities.

Parents often feel overwhelmed by the challenges associated with rearing a child with autism. Remember, you are the best parent for your child. You will be able to learn what you need to know, and you will receive spiritual impressions or intuitions to help you understand what to do for your child.

The ultimate goal as a parent is
to help your child improve and
one day obtain independence
so he can gain the freedom of
living on his own and
being successful in life.

For those with severe symptoms, it may never be possible for them to become independent enough to live on their own. They will either live with their parents or a trusted caregiver for the rest of their lives. For those who are able to gain independence, they may go on to use their talents to be successful. Remember, the way they are as children may not be the way they will be as adults.

How do we help them get there? The next chapters give an overview of services, therapies and treatment that are extremely beneficial in improving their development.

Why Should My Child Get a Diagnosis?

Hearing that your child has an ASD can feel like a truck ran you over. After the shock goes away, **a diagnosis can bring peace of mind and help you develop a vision and a plan to move forward toward success.** You don't have to have a diagnosis to receive therapy and services. However, **it clears up a lot of doubt and opens doors for services, treatment, and therapies that might not be available otherwise.**

If you think there is a concern, you are probably right. Trust your instincts as your child's parent. If someone recommends that your child get evaluated, it isn't going to hurt to do it.

Along with developmental delays or challenges, those with an ASD usually show gifted abilities in areas such as science, music, or art. These talents and abilities can be nurtured to bring about success and hope for their futures.

Sometimes other people may view your child's negative or unusual behaviors as a negative reflection on your parenting skills.

This is not true. Believing this falsehood leads to unwarranted parental guilt, which is a huge roadblock that can keep the child from receiving help. Guilt can get in the way of parents' need to accept the diagnosis and realize that their child has an atypical challenge that needs to be addressed.

The guilt parents feel when they accept others' uninformed judgments can also affect parents' confidence, thus preventing them from moving forward toward help or solutions.

In the case of my sons, I did not want them to be diagnosed, and I fought against it. When I educated myself more about the disorder, I changed my perspective. My boys needed help, and my husband and I could not provide for their needs alone. After I was willing to let go of my parental guilt and accept their diagnoses, I was able to get them the help they needed.

Don't see autism as a label that defines your child; instead, view it as an explanation of his challenges and strengths. If you had a child with a major health or medical issue, such as cancer, you would not hesitate to get him help. Take the opportunity to educate yourself and get a correct diagnosis.

I have just been told my child has autism. Is there any hope?

YES, THERE IS HOPE!

When you give children with autism the opportunities and tools to make improvements, they can be functional in life—without their emotional episodes and the challenges that can isolate them from others. Then they can use their amazing minds to benefit themselves and others. We don't want to get rid of the talents and gifts their minds are capable of, we want to channel those focused obsessions into bringing about good. Some with autistic minds have contributed to many great advancements in the sciences and in the technologies we use today. Their unique interests and focused attention to detail gives then the capacity to think on levels apart from those who are nero-typical, thus allowing their unique perspectives that have led to the invention of or development of some of our modern conveniences.

What Are the Symptoms of Autism?

Autistic symptoms can vary greatly from mild to severe, and include a wide range of differences in people's developmental abilities. When people are diagnosed with autism, they are described as having low-functioning (severe) autism, classic (moderate) autism, or high functioning (mild) autism. Some people confuse functional ability with IQ level. They are not the same. People with autism almost always have an IQ level that is higher than their functioning abilities. Any one of them could have a low IQ of less than 70 or an extremely high IQ of 140 or more. Often those with low functional abilities have a lower IQ than those with higher functional abilities. However there are some exceptions, such as when someone with severe autism is extremely intelligent but is unable to communicate well enough to display her brilliance.

It is a mistake to assume that one who is nonverbal has a low IQ. In recent years, technological devices have enabled those without verbal skills to communicate, and they are surprising everyone with how much they know. Speak to them as if they understand, with respect to their presence and feelings. They are more like you and I than we think.

Brief descriptions of the symptoms of autism are listed below. This is a summary of information provided by the National Institute of Health and *Autism Speaks*. I've also included information I have learned through my own experience. Please remember that a list of symptoms doesn't truly describe the depths or dynamics of what is happening. In addition, an individual might have periods of regression in his development. Remember, there is a wide range of delays; *an individual does not have to exhibit all of these symptoms, and the number of symptoms can vary from one person to another.*

Communication

- Is nonverbal or has delayed speech
- Struggles with to-and-fro conversation
- Repeats noises or phrases excessively, for instance, the child may repeat the last word or phrase spoken by someone else

over and over again, like a broken record (This repetitive behavior is called Echolalia.)

- Speaks in a monotone or in a loud voice
- Gives little or poor eye contact
- Is less responsive; may appear to be deaf
- Has limited interaction with others
- Laughs or cries for no apparent reason
- Unable to follow multiple directions
- Understands words literally, thinks literally, and does not understand sarcasm, innuendos, puns, or idioms

Social Skills

- Appears to be unresponsive to others' emotions or feelings
- Has difficulty expressing how he or she feels
- Uses little to no facial expressions
- Is awkward, immature or inappropriate in social settings
- Prefers to be alone, often in his or her "own world"
- Does not pick up on social cues
- Has limited interests, some to the point of obsession
- Is unaware of real danger

Behaviors

- Has repetitive behaviors such as hand flapping, hair twisting, verbal jargoning, tiptoe walking, rocking, spinning, or pacing
- Develops detailed routines or rituals
- Is disturbed by change; has difficulty making transitions
- Is physically over active or under active; may stand up, jump, or climb at random times.
- Plays or uses objects unusually, for example, spinning wheels, lining up toys or objects, or being obsessive over a certain toy or object
- Mouths, bites, or smells objects
- Exhibits self-injurious behavior such as head banging, biting, scratching, or pulling on skin
- Has big tantrums, meltdowns, or blowups over minor events such as things not being in a certain order, small transitions, or over stimulation of his senses

Inappropriate behaviors are manifestations of the child's frustrations or sensory overstimulation. Communication delays create a great deal of frustration because the child cannot express what he wants, and so his needs are not met. You can recognize when a child with autism is experiencing sensory overload; the child will either seek or avoid stimulation that excites one of the senses—touch, oral, vision, hearing, or smell. (Look for more details on sensory issues in chapter 2.)

Asperger syndrome is almost identical to high-functioning autism. Those with Asperger syndrome often do not have a significant speech or language delay before age three as do children with moderate to severe autism. They still have difficulty with to-and-fro conversation and can fixate over one topic. Most are interested in giving listeners an encyclopedia of information. Their social skills are awkward. They want to be a part of society but struggle to understand all the social graces. They often exhibit behavior at an age much younger than their years. Their behaviors are not as noticeable in a public setting and will appear to be neuro-typical, but if you spend a fair amount of time with them, you will notice a difference.

Pervasive Developmental Disorder—Not Otherwise Specified (PDD-NOS). This classification is used when a person shows impairments in communication, social skills, and behaviors, but does not meet the criteria for any of the other ASD groups. This is the mildest form of autism. But daily life is still a challenge. Managing anxiety, communication delays, social delays, and repetitive behaviors are a constant struggle. However, these challenges are not at the same degree of difficulty as those with classic autism.

Autistic savants are extremely gifted individuals who have unbelievable faculties. Approximately 10 percent of those with autism are gifted enough to be called savants. These brilliant individuals can have amazing abilities such as playing a song perfectly after hearing it only once, drawing a picture to detail having seen it only once, making amazing sculptures with their hands, having a photographic memory, or remembering a large amount of information about dates and times of specific events, weather, or facts. They may be able to calculate square roots and other difficult math problems in their heads quickly. Still, they struggle with the same developmental delays as others with autism.

The two rarest forms of autism are Rett syndrome and childhood disintegrative disorder. **Rett syndrome primarily affects girls and comes on after a period of normal development early in life. It is the most physically disabling of the ASD's.** The affects are extreme:

- Loss of speech
- Disordered breathing
- Disrupted sleep patterns
- Severe digestion problems
- Impaired heart and circulation
- Extreme anxiety
- Fragility in the bone structure, such as scoliosis
- Loss of motor control

- Hand functional abilities are replaced by compulsive hand movements
- Parkinsonian tremors
- Seizures

Rett syndrome has been linked to a specific gene, MECP2. It is the first of the ASD's to have a reversal seen in an animal (rats). This study was completed in 2007. Lack of funding has delayed continued research from developing a way to treat affected girls. (National Institute of Mental Health, Mayo Clinic Staff)

Childhood disintegrative disorder is found mostly in males. The child develops normally until the age of two to four years. The National Institute of Mental Health and the Mayo Clinic say that these children may also exhibit these symptoms:

- Loses a huge amount of speech
- Unable to talk or have a conversation
- Loses motor skills and the ability to walk, climb, and hold on to objects
- Struggles with social skills; can't relate to or interact with others
- Loss of bladder and bowel control, even after previously being potty trained
- May have seizures
- Can have a low IQ.

That Boy Is so Smart; How Could He Have Autism?

Children with autism have challenges, but they also have strengths. Some are gifted in math, art, science, or have amazing memories and can pay attention to detail. They can be extremely focused on a topic they are interested in or remember facts and information that others find difficult to recall. Some can decode language without knowing how to speak or write it. They can also be honest, almost to a fault.

They are obsessed over details and have the ability to focus their attention on figuring things out, even if that means they forget to bathe or eat and lose track of time. They are the geniuses who think concretely, so music, science, art, and technology often comes very naturally to them.

Researchers believe Mozart had a form of autism. His teachers thought he was a lost cause. He isolated himself and had behavioral issues, but he was excellent at playing the piano and violin and at composing music. We can thank many gifted individuals, who also happened to have autism for so many of our advancements in music, science, art, and technology. (Fitzgerald)

Chapter 2

Sensory Processing
and the Challenge of Change

Shopping with children with autism can be extremely challenging. They are bombarded with an overload of senses to process, and their filters to block out these senses do not work as they should. Try to understand the depth of their distress and imagine not being able to filter all the senses you process every day.

Imagine being a child with autism at the supermarket: A squeaky wheel on the cart is making an annoying noise. Plus there is a constant beeping from the checkout stands. You cover your ears to try and block out the rushing flood of sounds pounding in your ears. The florescent lightbulbs are buzzing and strobing light across the store, making it hard to see. You feel dizzy and shake your head to try and make things clear, but the fish department and the detergent isle have a flood of smells that get stuck in your nose, like if someone had sprayed every perfume at the counter in the department store directly in your face. Then someone makes an announcement on the overhead speaker about today's specials. It's so loud and scary; you want to jump out of your skin. A person walking by brushes your arm; it sends a zing from your scalp to your toes.

This sensory overload is causing you distress. Your anxiety level has risen to the point of panic. It's all too much. All you can do to make it stop is to have a meltdown, to cry, or to blow up. Screaming or throwing a tantrum will help you block out the other noises and the terrifying wave of senses. That way you only hear yourself, and you hope that the world will stop and be still and quiet for a few minutes so you can escape your imprisonment.

Now imagine you are the parent of the child with autism in this situation. People are staring and looking on with judgment. Someone dares to say, "Would you control your child?" Another asks, "What's wrong with him?" It's all you can do to calm your child down, in an effort to prevent his behavior from escalating into hitting, biting, or running away. You are embarrassed over what everyone else is thinking, because experience has taught you to expect these responses from others.

You do your best to stay calm, because you don't want your child to feed off the bystanders' negative reactions. You struggle to pick your child up off the floor, hoping your tears don't start falling until after you manage to get to the car. You fight back the building anger that accompanies the sadness and wonder how you are ever going to be able to go shopping again.

Some parents use humor to handle the stress and embarrassment they feel when their child acts out, and they may address the "gawkers."

I charge by the minute,
if you want to keep looking.

– Laura

I say, "Could you give us some space?"

What Are Sensory Challenges?

One day I asked my eight-year-old son, "Why do you flap your hands?"

He responded, "They are numb. They are asleep, so I am waking them up."

The brain requires both hemispheres to connect. When they are out of balance, Sensory messages are missed or delayed. We all have a level of tolerance to things that stimulate our senses, but **those with autism have hypo- or hypersensitivities**, **meaning they avoid or seek out sensory input.** Individuals with autism have difficulty processing sensory input, and so when there is an overload of one or more senses it can bring about discomfort or pain. The following shows a variety of possible discomforts:

- This overload often brings on an outburst of emotions and behaviors.
- The level of sensory tolerance in an individual with autism is less than the average person.
- To those with noise sensitivities, it can feel like it will rupture the ear drums, or the noise can bring on a headache.
- Touch can feel sharp or very uncomfortable.
- Visually, something might look out of place to someone with autism. If a pattern is "broken," this can cause distress.
- Smell can make a person with autism feel nauseated.
- Some explore objects with their mouths.
- Others may bang their head in response to overloaded sensory.

- Some may have impaired spatial awareness. To compensate, they may spin in circles, flap their hands, or tip toe walk.

How Can We Help Children with Autism When They Are Overstimulated?

Notice to what triggers them and try to make necessary adjustments. For us as parents, it can be so overwhelming when our child behaves in odd ways to compensate for his or her overload. Sometimes we can't figure out what the trigger is, and it leaves us guessing. Learning more about what can be triggers for others can help us figure out the triggers in our own kids. Here are some examples of how it is for some. As you read, keep in mind that those with autism may not have every sense affected.

Touch

A child with autism may invade your personal space and touch everything he sees. He may touch the front of someone's shirt or the back of someone's pants because of his curiosity about the pattern or texture of the fabric.

I constantly find finger marks in foods because of my son's obsession to touch. He explores through touch and seeks satisfaction through that sense. Our sons, like so many others, become very attached to favorite toys or objects, including clothing that often become a permanent part of their attire for an atypical length of time. A certain superhero costume is currently in hiding at our house because one of our boys would wear it all day long and then go to bed in it—for days on end. For a couple months he fought us almost every time we needed him to take it off to take a bath or to go to the bathroom.

Another child may not want to be touched or hugged. Shirt tags, the type of fabric (such as denim), the texture of the fabric, or the position of the clothing can be irritating. It might bring so much discomfort that he takes off his shoes and socks or strips down to almost nothing so he'll feel relief.

Other children may like wearing their clothing in ways that seem unusual to us. The texture, position, or tightness of the clothing may need to be adjusted or changed. One of our sons likes to wear his pants higher than or just below his belly button, with his belt pulled as tightly as possible. His shoes are laced tightly and his socks and pulled up just so. It is very difficult for him to do a task until his clothing is fixed in the way he feels comfortable. I remember him screaming as a young toddler because the seam of his sock was pressing against his toes. It took multiple tries to get the sock comfortable enough, and he often made us late for an event.

Combing, brushing, cutting hair, and other grooming necessities can be a nightmare. The buzzing of the clippers, the pull of the hair from the scalp, or the water drops falling on their face, shoulders, or arms all create an overwhelming sensory experience that the child will resist with all energy he can muster. Going to the salon was not worth the money—Teaching stylists how to cut the hair of child with autism isn't exactly in the cosmetology lesson manual. So we learned to do it ourselves. We learned to play games and have several distractions in order to get the grooming done. At times my husband and I have had to resort to holding our boys' heads still while the other cuts off the hair as fast as possible so the trauma will be over quickly and so the boys will look somewhat decent. It is a blessing that they are all boys. We at least had the option to cut their hair really short until they had gained some personal grooming skills.

Some people with autism experience other irritating sensations. Their skin may feel like it's on fire or like spiders are crawling all over them. To make these unpleasant sensations go away, they may jump up and down repeatedly.

Some may develop phobias to germs, which can become a major hindrance in daily living.

Hot and cold temperatures in a room can also affect them.

We can have empathy for how those with autism may feel when we recall times when we felt physically miserable ourselves. Think of a time when you had a fever, felt achy all over, had hives, or had extra-sensitive skin.

Seasonal changes and changes in air pressure affect many of those with autism. During these times they might become irritable and unable to communicate what they are feeling. Their irritation may escalate to banging their heads against the floor or wall to try and bring relief. Their anxieties can get so bad that they bite themselves or others.

In our family, we do activities that are fun and relaxing for our boys and that help lower their anxieties to touch. For instance, we have used blankets to wrap our boys up like "pigs in a blanket" and then squeezed them by giving them bear hugs. We also bounce an exercise ball up and down their bodies while they are wrapped in a blanket. Our youngest loves to be swung in his blanket. In order to regulate his anxiety levels, another son often rubs his eyes and pulls on his eyebrows.

Oral

Certain textures of food can be a problem for some with autism. **When people with autism have an oral fixation, they may reject a certain food because of how it feels in their mouths.** They may only want certain foods. Some may like foods that are chewy or crunchy such as corn nuts, pretzels, gummy bears, or licorice because they stimulate their jaws. Others avoid certain colors, like red, and will only eat whitish-colored foods. **Some, wanting to stimulate their oral senses, may lick the walls, eat dirt, or put everything in their mouths, including unsafe objects.** Since most people with autism have no sense of danger, they may even ingest toxic substances.

Toys and tools have been developed to help with oral fixations. Therapeutic chew toys, chewlery (bracelets, necklaces, or other jewelry that is designed for chewing), other oral tools (such as P's and Q's), and certain foods can help satisfy the drive to put things in their mouths and chew on them.

Vision

Not being able to predict others' movements can bring on feelings of anxiety in some children. Others might not be able to handle bright lights or even bright sunlight. Others are distressed by bright colors. Florescent light bulbs can cause a pulsing strobe effect and make it difficult for some children to even see at all. In addition, florescent lights make a constant buzzing noise that their sensitive ears may hear. If you can, get rid of florescent light bulbs in your home.

On the other hand, some may be mesmerized by what they see. They might seek sight stimulation and want to watch fast moving objects—either in person or on television or in movies.

Others with autism "think in pictures," in other words, when they see an object or hear a word, their mind immediately recalls all of the "pictures" in their mind about similar objects. Temple Grandin has this ability. For instance, if she sees a shoe, her mind may then recall and flash pictures of the hundreds of shoes she has seen in her life. Because of this, some individuals avoid eye contact. This helps them to minimize the endless stream of pictures that comes to their minds when looking at someone, creating a train of thoughts and pictures flashing into their mind. (*Thinking in Pictures*, 24, 73)

Eye contact can also be difficult for other reasons. Those with autism can appear to be completely disengaged because they are staring off into space, at the wall, or not paying attention to others around them. However they are likely paying attention to every detail of your face and being so attentive to those features that they don't make eye contact.

Despite these difficulties, it is important to continue working with children who do not want to make eye contact, teaching them this essential social and communication skill.

Those with autism often stare at objects such as curtains, walls, or windows. They are fascinated by the patterns they see or by the way a room or piece of furniture looks.

They can be compulsive about always clearing the table or tossing couch throw pillows onto the floor. They want a table to look like a *table* or a couch to look like a *couch.* To them, "clutter" (such as dishes on a table or pillows on a couch) changes the way the object looks so that, to them, it no longer looks like a table or a couch.

They might also line up their toys or objects in order of importance or organize them by size or color. They may get very upset if you move any of the items out of order.

Hearing

If you have ever had a severe headache, you know how painful noise can be. Parties, reunions, arcades, theaters, assemblies, and amusement parks are all filled with noise. **Individuals with autism may avoid loud noises because it hurts their ears and brings on a feeling of panic**. To try to block out their panic and feelings of overload, some children might cover their ears, shake their heads, or rock back and forth. Or they might compensate by talking really loudly or continually chattering. Some end up having a meltdown because the noise is causing so much distress.

When it gets loud
it feels like there is pressure
all around me, and I feel trapped.

— Tyler

You can help a child who is overwhelmed by sound. You can put earmuffs over his ears to help minimize the noise, or you can give him headphones plugged into an MP3 player to distract him from the noise that distresses him. You can also take him out of the environment or go for a walk to give him time to desensitize.

Our youngest will grab my hands and motion for me to put them on his ears. He really likes it if I gently squeeze his head while covering his ears. This gentle squeeze comforts him and helps him to cope. Without my help, he resorts to unusual or damaging behaviors such as stiffening up his head and hands and then shaking until he relieves the pressure. As he gets older, we will teach him how to cover and squeeze his own ears instead of doing the negative behaviors.

Smell

Odors can make a child with smell sensitivities feel very uncomfortable—much like many women feel when they are pregnant and have a bionic sense of smell. Odors can make the child feel like she can't breathe or that she is nauseated. She may have difficulty blocking out perfumes and fragrances, detergents, body odor, cigarettes, smoke from fireworks and campfires, fish, or eggs. It becomes very difficult for her to focus on anything else. This hyper aversion to some smells often translates into eating difficulties since smell affects taste. Imagine eating something that smells nasty to you. You would avoid foods with those smells too.

Depending on the level of discomfort, I can be distracted or downright incapacitated by smells.

– Fiona

The opposite happens as well. A child may enjoy smelling things. He may smell everything—his food, clothing, people, places, everything he touches or picks up. This can become an obsessive behavior. My son is very aware and often comments if there is a good or bad smell in our home.

Balance

Some children with autism feel anxious or overwhelmed because their vestibular senses (sense of balance) are distorted.

They may experience dizziness, a loss of balance, nausea, or distorted hearing or vision. This can make doing everyday activities or athletics seem impossible. He may fall off a chair or stool easily, trip over his own feet or have trouble with stairs.

Spatial Awareness

Spatial awareness is the sense of feeling when you are in the air or space around you. **When a child's spatial awareness is out of balance, he may spin in circles, run into walls, or jump off furniture, all to seek deep pressure stimulation in order to feel himself in space.** This behavior can go on for hours each day.

He may also struggle with pencil holding, writing, using a spoon or fork, or doing other fine-motor-skill activities. Both the lack of balance and spatial awareness can go unnoticed by adults, leaving the child in a scary environment. And since communication is often difficult, he is unable to tell his caregiver how he feels.

If you are new to autism, you may question the behaviors you might see as a child with autism is spinning, jumping up and down, screaming, flapping his hands, covering his ears, talking to himself or doing some other awkward, or inappropriate or aggressive behavior and wonder, "Why?" Talk to his parents or a sensory therapist to gain a better understanding about the specific sensory processing challenges he faces. Learn what will help him in those difficult situations. Understand that sometimes even the parents don't know all that is going on with their child's senses. Parents and professional are a great team in figuring out what sensory challenges need to be addressed and how to bring balance to the child's senses.

Many children with autism need (and demand) absolute consistency in their environment.

Transitions

Transitions can be difficult adjustments for those with autism. They might blow up because you ended something early or switched the order of the day's activities. The challenges of these anxieties are difficult for caregivers to manage and are major hindrances to their ability to focus on schoolwork, to remember what to say in a conversation, or how to behave appropriately. Others allow their anxiety to build all day and then come home where they feel safe and finally let it go, resulting in a major blow up or melt down.

My friend Fiona describes the challenge she faces with her son during normal transitions, such as when they move from a school schedule to a summer schedule. "Schedules and lists are my coping mechanism for transition troubles," she says. "Those with ASD have trouble moving from one activity to another or from one thought to another. Schedules and lists give order and structure and make those transitions easier to manage and sometimes possible when they would otherwise be impossible.

"As an adult I feel pulled in so many directions," she continues, "and even if I do make a plan, of course it will change. Priorities are in a constant flux. By the end of the day, my life is often so topsy turvy that I am either too high strung from all the input, or I am brain-dead and can't process the simplest thing.

"Last summer, I devised a three-hour-a-day summer school schedule for my son with Asperger. I typed it up and presented it to him, quite proud of meeting his need for schedules.

"He studied it, and then asked, 'But what are we doing in the afternoon?'

"'Oh, that is when you do your chores and practicing,' I said.

"'But it isn't on the schedule!' he said.

" So, I put it on the schedule.

"'What about night and morning?' he asked

"So I went back to the drawing board to make a summer schedule that had every minute accounted for from waking to bedtime. My son was okay with the fact that at least two hours a day said FREE TIME. It just had to be on the schedule."

Children are comforted by order and schedules. The consistency helps to lower their anxieties, which in turn helps keep the home feeling calm and peaceful. However, it's good now and then to throw in a planned change to help them know what to do for those times when life throws unpredictability their way. But be prepared and have ideas to teach them how to manage that change. It will be difficult at first but with repetition it can become easier. Practicing will teach them how to make transitions and how to be calmer about change.

What Simple Techniques Can I Use to Help Calm or Soothe a Child with Autism?

Provide a calm and structured environment, void of overloaded stimuli: soft lighting, low volume, neutral smells, and a small number of people. If you are caring for someone on a regular basis, learn what her schedule is and what therapy methods are used to help her. If she doesn't have any yet, here are some that you can try *with parental approval.*

- Give her advanced notice that change is coming, or learn what helps her make transitions.
- Apply appropriate deep massage pressure by squeezing the arms or legs in a downward motion. Start from the shoulders and move down to the fingers (or from the mid-thighs to the toes), making sure both sides are equally massaged. The back may be massaged, but avoid the stomach or chest.
- Roll her up in a blanket like a burrito or hot dog, then squeeze her or give her bear hugs or bounce a ball up and down her back.
- Have her wear a weighted backpack, a vest, or a blanket.
- Play Mozart and other calming music.
- Use chew toys or tools to help with oral senses (see previous section on oral senses.)
- Brush her and apply joint compressions. (Learn this therapy exercise from a professional.)
- Implement cross-brain activities that connect right and left sides of the brain, such as jumping jacks, swinging, rocking,

jumping on a mini trampoline, doing puzzles, and constructing and building toys. Avoid television and movies when possible, because they do not help her brain function. However, don't discard them altogether; there are many times when media entertainment is necessary to give a caregiver a little downtime or a well deserved break.

- When a behavior escalates beyond your control, let her be alone in a safe place. She will calm down. **Only restrain the child if you are trained to do so or when authorities have asked you to do it.**

He may laugh or cry
for no apparent reason,
until he is inconsolable.
Something has triggered his behavior;
look for it.

One of my favorite examples of what the child and parent go through is found in the movie *Temple Grandin,* which accurately portrays what life was like for Dr. Temple Grandin when she was young. It gets to the heart of what those with autism feel and struggle with. At the end of the movie, Temple is at an autism conference and describes what it is like to have autism. It also shows the demands autism places on the family. Most importantly, the movie gives hope as it shows how Temple pursued her unique interests by using her strengths to be successful in life. I highly recommend watching the entire movie and the extras with Temple's commentary because of its unique insights into the world of autism. It won seven Emmy Awards, and Claire Danes won the Golden Globe Award for her role as Temple.

Chapter 3

Improving the Quality of Life:
Services and Therapy Information

Autism can seem invisible at times.
One moment she is behaving
like a typical child and
the next, she is not.

Behavioral Challenges

Behavioral challenges aren't just a struggle for the child, but are also difficult for those who live with her and who are in the line of fire during difficult behavioral episodes. Parents work hard to manage their child's behaviors. They try to stop her from damaging property or hurting herself or others with her aggressive behavior.

Typical parenting techniques do not work with a challenging child and often only add to the child's behavioral challenges. If you use anger, lectures, threats, or warnings, it will be a waste of your time. Whenever we used anger, it only increased the fear of an already terrified and sensory-overloaded child. He was not able to hear anything we said, and the threats and warnings became empty. Learn advanced parenting skills that teach you what to do in order to help your challenged child be calm and survive the daily chaos.

The first time my husband and I responded calmly to one of our son's routine outbursts and saw how effective it was, we couldn't help but laugh. It felt so good to be in control of the situation and to be handling it successfully. This experience changed how we looked at our sons' behaviors. It became so much easier to take control when our energy was not spent on our reactions and being caught up in the drama; we could use that energy to come up with creative ways to handle the next "performance."

When you mentally step
outside of the situation,
you can be objective and even laugh
at your child's annoying behaviors.

— Janice

Parents and professionals can work together to identify the child's triggers. Look for sensory overloads, physical or medical conditions, or emotional triggers. Does the child jump onto an emotional rollercoaster over minor frustrations or discouragements? Are his senses being irritated? Does he have food allergies or does he eat only a select number of foods? How often is he in a state of panic or anxiety? Does he have sleep disruptions, digestive issues, or other illnesses? What examples of poor behavior are in his environment?

Brain Function

In 2003, 33 of the leading doctors, research scientists, and mental health and youth service professionals for children in the United States met to discuss concerns about the growing numbers of children and teens in the U.S. who have emotional distress or mental health or behavioral problems. Their report, *Hardwired to Connect*, stated we humans are hardwired to attach or connect to others and to a higher power. Trauma, illness, or lack of nurturing damages the shape and circuits of the brain, creating high levels of stress and anxiety that affect our behaviors, emotions, and mental state. This increases our vulnerability to depression, social isolation, and mental health issues. **These professionals concluded that our connections or attachments to others are at the root of all mental illnesses and disorders.** (YMCA of USA, et. al)

Trauma or high amounts of anxiety can damage the brain.

Anxiety causes even neuro-typical people to react with survival instincts—flight, fight, and freeze. People suffering from high amounts of anxiety may have heightened senses, a difficult time sleeping, improper organ function, and illogical behavior. For those with autism, there are additional disconnections in the brain that cause even more dysfunction. Parts of the brain may overdevelop (which is why those with autism have gifted abilities), while other areas of the brain such as those that process facial recognition and communication are underdeveloped. In addition, the constant anxieties associated with having an autistic brain make it even more challenging for it to make new connections. Thus sensory overload, anxiety, and brain dysfunction often result in behavioral issues that can become extreme for the child and overwhelming for the family.

Dr. W. Dean Belnap explains the serious affect on the brain and body due to high amounts of anxiety and stress. He says when a person is in a state of anxiety, cortisol—a natural chemical in the brain— is released to help the person survive. It heightens the individual's senses and makes him more vigilant—much like animal instincts. "The normal brain has a cybernating rhythm that cycles the entire brain at the average rate of 9 to 10 cycles per second. Under stress, that rhythm often cycles to 20 [to] 25 per second. This is fatiguing to the brain, particularly to the frontal cortex." (Belnap)

When too much cortisol is released, in a constant high state of alert—especially in children, Dr. Belnap explains—this can have permanent adverse effects on the brain. The brain shuts down the frontal lobes, causing the individual to become unable to think clearly. The frontal lobe is the part of the brain that controls reasoning, moral judgment, and emotional understanding. This impairment results in the survival instincts (basil ganglia) taking control of the brain. **The large amount of continuous flow of cortisol in the brain results in mental illness caused by chronic stress and anxiety. Functional MRIs have shown the lack of activity in the frontal cortex of those who have experienced long-term anxiety and in more serious cases, there is actually a loss of brain tissue.** Just like a computer, if a wire is shorted out or disconnected, it is not going to work properly. (Belnap)

Studies show that if the brain becomes accustomed to large amounts of cortisol, it begins to crave it, and cortisol becomes a natural addiction for the brain. Subconsciously, the individual begins to want cortisol rushes. Thus individuals, including those with autism, may subconsciously create situations that will feed that cortisol "addiction." This is similar to adrenaline junkies who constantly seek for "the rush" by jumping out of planes or doing other risky behaviors. (Belnap)

High amounts of anxiety contribute to sleep deprivation and gastrointestinal problems, which is a common issue with ASD's. Organs shut down when in a state of fight or flight. When the brain is stuck in survival mode, serotonin is not being released. Serotonin has an effect opposite that of cortisol. Serotonin is needed to help bring balance to brain function. The brain needs enough serotonin to create the melatonin needed to help you fall asleep and stay asleep.

To lower high levels of cortisol in the brain, engage in activities such as exercising, yoga, getting a massage, laughing, crying, and listening to music; such as Mozart. Research has also found omega-3' fatty acids and vitamin-C to help as well. It would also be wise to avoid caffeine, sleep deprivation, intense exercise, severe trauma, or stressful events which only increase the level of cortisol in the brain.

Behavioral Therapies

When messages in the brain are not connecting correctly there is brain dysfunction. Parts of the brain are not "firing" as they should to relay messages. **Brain function and behavioral therapies, such as sensory integration, brain gym, horse therapy, attachment therapy, and applied behavioral analysis (ABA),**

build hemispheric connections in the brain. These therapies can help significantly improve a person's behavior, communication, and social skills. These therapies work at addressing the individual's anxieties and are a major key in helping to build brain function by creating hemispheric connections in the brain. Therapy also improves developmental skills such as eye contact, communication and increases their desire to be engaged with others. In therapy the levels of cortisol and serotonin become balanced and the fight, flight or freeze responses are significantly reduced.

Sensory Therapy

The goal of sensory therapy is to develop an individual's sensory diet; it addresses seek and avoid issues in a healthy and manageable way. Many people mistake a sensory diet to mean a nutrition diet. Instead , a sensory diet works to balance out the individual's hypo- and hypersensitivities to the senses. This helps to lower his anxieties and improve his developmental skills. A sensory diet is only food related if the child has a sensory challenge with eating. The book, *The Out-of-Sync Child*, describes sensory issues and helps you recognize your child's sensory processing challenges. *The Out-of-Sync Child Has Fun* teaches you how to develop a sensory diet.

A psychiatrist or physician may recommend finding an occupational therapist that specializes in sensory therapies. At rehabilitation facilities you can find knowledgeable sensory therapists that help you better understand your child's sensory challenges. They will teach you what to do to help with your child's sensory needs. School districts often have an occupational therapy (OT) specialist at the school at least once week who can work with your child for a limited amount of time. OT services at schools are not guaranteed. The services may be found at a rehabilitation clinic, but most will not be free.

We enjoyed going to a rehabilitation center to try out the abundant tools and equipment and to watch how our youngest son responded to them before purchasing them ourselves. We found that activities such as push and pull, climbing and crashing, and swinging and jumping all satisfied his craving for deep pressure sensations. We have incorporated what we learned for all of our boys' sensory needs.

It is wonderful how calm and refocused our boys get when they do 20 or 30 jumping jacks. I have even had teachers implement jumping jacks at school, and they are amazed at how well it works. Jumping jacks are a great cross-brain activity that helps calm and self-regulate our boys' anxieties. We do this both on the floor and on the mini-tramp. Jumping jacks help them to self-regulate their anxiety. Our sons are more willing and able to follow directions because the exercise has shifted their thinking from survival mode to logical thinking. We tell them their exercises are shifting their brains from "stop" to "go".

Brain Gym

Brain gym is exercise that works both sides of the body: Exercise such as jumping on a mini-trampoline, jumping jacks, and balancing, all build hemispheric connections. This can be done at home once the equipment and training have been acquired.

When we see our boys' behaviors deteriorate, we say phrases like "Get your brain in gear and jump on your tramp," or "Give me 20 jumping jacks." Then after the exercise, we can ask them, "What happened?" About 90 percent of the time, they can say—with clarity—what their behavior was and what they will do differently next time.

It takes a lot of training, patience, and practice to implement brain gym. During the first few months our boys threw major tantrums as we practiced brain exercises with them, but after they were used to it, they enjoyed it. So don't get discouraged while implementing brain exercises. Keep trying.

Horse Therapy

Horse therapy (equine therapy) is brain gym magnified. This therapy works to re-pattern the individual's brain and rebuild the right and left hemisphere connections that are out of balance or not functioning. It facilitates the connection between the frontal lobes and the right and the left sides of the brain. The horse also helps individual's process the emotions, that are difficult for those with autism to identify and express.

Hippotherapy is also done with a horse and requires that an occupational, physical, or speech and language therapist is present during the session.

During horse therapy, the horse gives neuro-feedback by instinctively mirroring the rider's emotions. The horse will exhibit a behavior similar to the rider's true emotion. During our boys' horseback rides, the horses have tried to run away, bite, buck, invade personal space, or stubbornly stand still reflecting the behaviors our boys' will do at home. (Despite the horse's behaviors, the child is safe because the horse is being managed by a professional.)

The feedback from the horses shows the rider's neurological state. This gives the instructor or therapist the information needed during the session to help balance the connections in the rider's brain help then to and process their emotions. By processing their emotions' while on the horse, our sons' then have minimal outbursts or meltdowns and are able to regain control of their emotional behavior.

All of our boys have shown improvements with horse therapy. They make better eye contact, have more interaction with others, experience fewer emotional episodes, communicate better, and are calmer and happier. Our youngest struggles with delayed communication and has had several speech regressions. After several months of riding, he began communicating in small three- to four-word sentences and began retaining more.

We've discovered that each hippotherapy ride is a different experience. Almost two years later, it still continues to help our boys develop and improve.

Look for a facility that specializes in working with those who have mental disorders and disabilities. You want a place that has quality docile horses such as the Missouri Fox Trotter or Fjord, which have a long and smooth gait (walk) and that has the necessary therapy saddles that allow the rider to feel the movements of the horse. Also look for a facility that knows how to work on brain patterning, emotional processing and trust exercises. Some horse therapy centers do not work primarily with clients who have special needs and do not work with younger children. Be selective of where you go for horse therapy, and be sure the personnel are knowledgeable and equipped to work with your child.

As we searched for a qualified facility, we observed and contacted several locations that offered horse therapy. However, their focus was on horsemanship and simple brain exercises rather than helping the rider improve brain function and process emotions. We finally found a facility, Hoofbeats to Healing, that meets the specifications of advanced horse therapy for our boys. Hoofbeats' focus is on reconnecting neurological dysfunctions. Contact information is found in the resource list at the end of the book. In the near future, Brigham Young University has plans to do a scientific research study at Hoofbeats to Healing. Using functional MRI's, they will document the patterning and connections in the brains of riders with neurological dysfunction.

Laura has a daughter with severe autism. She has seen amazing results from horse therapy. "Horse therapy has changed our lives," she says. "It has broken the shell of imprisonment for our daughter, unlocking her world and making her a part of our world. Four to five months after therapy began, she hugged me for the first time, and REALLY HUGGED ME (that is she initiated the hug.) I knew horse therapy was working and that we would do it for her lifetime. It is a regularly scheduled therapy that will be a constant in her life. For the first time she is now interacting with her grandparents, siblings, cousins, and other loved ones. The horses at Hoofbeats to Healing are healing her. She loves the horses. and we will be forever grateful."

Attachment Therapy

Attachment therapy has benefitted our boys' development as well. During our search to find out why two of our boys had behavioral challenges, one of our specialists suggested that they might have reactive attachment disorder (RAD). Autism and RAD have parallel symptoms. We began treating the behavioral problems using attachment therapy with a child therapist and a behavioral school. My husband and I were amazed how beneficial attachment therapy was for our boys.

Attachment therapy works towards healing the brain and bonding the individual with his mother and father, and shifting the brain from a survival state to a calm and logical state. It incorporates building eye contact, respect, and trust. It was a blessing in minimizing and stopping aggressive behavior that caused the whole family stress and anxiety. It involves advanced parenting skills and brain-building exercises as tools to help them make brain connections and focus their attention.

We saw a huge difference in our boys' behaviors and overall functional abilities after almost six months of consistently using attachment therapy. Over time, this advanced parenting became second nature for us. We continue implementing what we have learned even after our boys received a correct diagnosis of autism because it was so effective. You can find more information and a qualified therapist at www.attachment.org.

All behaviors serve a function
and have a purpose.
If benefits did not result
from displaying certain behaviors,
then individuals would stop doing them.

– Unknown

Behavior Plans

Behavior plans are used for those with behavioral challenges. These challenges stem from an overload of sensory issues, frustrations from communication struggles, or manipulating others to get what they want. Understand that these children are capable of using their challenges to get their way. It's good to have a clear understanding of what triggers the child's behaviors and determine what is a "can't" or "won't" situation. Often as caregivers, we give into our child's misbehaviors in order to avoid dealing with the challenges the behaviors create.

Many teachers and parents have had great success improving challenging behaviors in children by using applied behavioral analysis (ABA) therapy. ABA is an intense therapy with multiple levels of internalization that build upon each other. It focuses on documenting the course of behaviors and bridging gaps of communication and challenging the child to respond at a higher level of communication than he was previously capable of. He must respond to what the therapist is asking before he earns an incentive or reward. Many children, who were once unable to be in a regular classroom setting have become mainstreamed after implementing ABA therapy soon after diagnosis.

Talk with a team of professionals and find a behavior plan that addresses brain-building functions, communications, anxieties, and sensory challenges. Find out what works best for your child. As exhausting as it is, the result of parents and professionals consistently applying the same approach can significantly improve the child's behaviors. If your child's behaviors become worse in the beginning, it is a good indication that the therapy is working.

When behavioral problems are present, they become a huge roadblock in development. My boys' aggressive and sneaky behaviors drained me of all my energy and then some. It took several months of implementing new parenting techniques along with unwavering consistency before our boys stopped resisting the behavior plan and began to make improvements.

Simply avoiding anxieties or giving into bad behavior is not the answer. It takes advanced parenting and therapy to help the child achieve appropriate behaviors. This requires a large amount of patience and time from everyone who is involved with the child, because it will take a long time before there will be lasting improvements.

> *Regardless of punishment,*
> *a behavior is likely to happen again*
> *unless the underlying causes are*
> *identified and addressed.*
>
> *– Unknown*

Creative Solutions to Behavioral Challenges

During our training for advanced parenting techniques, it was insightful to know that yelling and screaming when we were beyond frustration only fed our sons' bad behavior and shifted their brains back into survival mode.

When behavior problems begin, you have only a small window in which to redirect your child. Otherwise, he is not going to understand you and anything you say. To him, you will sound like the adult characters in the *Peanuts* cartoon: "Wha wha wha wha, wha wha." It is only when your child is calm that you are able to communicate with him—giving him short instructions and brief lessons on social graces and appropriate behaviors.

We learned to respond and not react, to use action instead of anger or words. Now, when our sons misbehave, I no longer react with anger or frustration; instead, with a calm and determined voice, I say, "Thanks for letting me know that you would like to calm down in your room." Often, he would yell and sometimes hit.

When needed, I required him to make restitution for his behavior. Then if he chose not to go to his room, I said, "I'll be glad to start your time out when you are in your room and being calm." Sometimes I need to gently escort him to his room. When this situation repeated itself many times in a day, I would not say a word and only respond with action.

If my son's behavior becomes very aggressive, I remove the other children and myself until he is calm. He can throw a tantrum for a good hour before he calms down. After he is calm, I begin timing him for about five minutes. After a few minutes of calm I talk to him about what happened with short, black and white lessons. Now it rarely takes an hour for him to calm down. I quietly acknowledge his good behavior by saying, "You did it. You calmed down," while giving him a hug. Finally, he is required to give restitution and an apology when he is ready, before he can continue playing.

Now our son rarely hits, and if he does, it is not a fight to get him to his room. He is learning appropriate behavior that he will need in his real life outside of our home. There are still periods of relapses or regression, but it is still a big improvement.

To reach a new level of internalization it takes a LOT of repetition for a child with autism. Remember some individuals with autism have delayed responses and need more time than the average person to respond to what has been said. If you call the child by her name before you begin giving her instructions, it helps her brain to register that she needs to pay attention.

Even if you're on the right track,
you'll get run over if you just sit there.

– Will Rogers
(Brainy Quote)

Many parents, teachers, and even children with autism allow the diagnosis to be an excuse for bad behaviors or to set unnecessary limitations on the child. They will make excuses such as "Oh, he has autism: He can't do that." Or "Just let her do *this* so she will stop doing *that*." **Do not mistakenly substitute pity and pampering for respect and understanding. Have a clear understanding of their limitations and strengths. But don't accept their disability as an**

excuse for bad behavior, laziness, or manipulation. This assumption will stop them from improving.

Remember, children with autism are more like you than you think. Keep an open perspective and make observations. Teach them how to work through their anxieties rather than setting up an environment to avoid dealing with them. Recognize and acknowledge their achievements, coach them, and give them support and encouragement.

Rise to meet these behavioral challenges. **There are days when I am worn out and have nothing left because I have dug so deeply to get through the last hour.** My wonderful husband helps with the boys and provides opportunities for me so that I can give myself a break. I read, go for a walk, exercise, talk to a friend, laugh, sleep, write in my journal, listen to music. get a massage, watch a movie, or focus on strengthening my spirituality. I come back when I am recharged so I that I'll have the energy, patience, and willingness to get back to being a mom. We have also been blessed to have a respite provider come a couple of times a month to help give me and my husband additional breaks.

Autism + Humor = Sanity
I have to find the humor in the chaos
so I can keep myself sane.

– Laura

If your child has a difficult time being touched, create a playful environment that doesn't induce extreme anxiety or pain, but will make interactions with others less stressful. He will encounter random touches in his life, and this is good to practice. Do not tell him you are going to touch him. He will probably throw a fit, when you begin touching him without warning, but if you are expecting this reaction, you can plan accordingly. Randomly hug him by pretending you are a teddy bear or a monkey who wants to play with his ears. If it is a struggle, help open his arms to hug friends or family. Then acknowledge and praise him for trying and succeeding at making another step closer to his goal.

Our son screams like his arm has just been cut off whenever he is bumped or scratched. So, we play along with his theatrics and prescribe a "cure" we tell him, "You need to rest all day in bed because you're hurt. Don't worry about watching your favorite movie today, you can watch it when you are feeling better. Oh, and I will be happy to bring you some chicken soup so you can get better." It's a miracle! All of a sudden he feels better! Oh, but he will still be taking a rest in his bed. Because of my consistency in the past, he knows I will follow through the next time he screams over a minor incident. His sensitivities to touch do not need to result in bad behaviors. Allowing it to continue would only create a bigger struggle for him to overcome in the future.

When you know she struggles with certain events that trigger anxieties, help her practice before the event comes. That way she can be familiar with what to do and know what to expect. For instance practice going to the store for a short period of time, and then work up to a longer trip. If she has a positive and successful experience at an event that was once extremely stressful, it can help her to see that it is possible to do it again and again. Then as other opportunities for experiences come, the next transition or event will be easier to overcome.

When a new behavioral plan is introduced, you will know it is working if he resists at first (which could be a few days to a few months).

Toilet training can be a HUGE struggle, and it can take a considerable amount of time for him to master, if he masters it at all. Also, hygiene and self care can be a stinky issue (or worse) in his adolescence. At some point in adolescence, he will decide for himself to be responsible or become determined to be more like his peers. He may do it with innocent awkwardness, but use that to introduce proper hygiene and to have fun with him. Never embarrass him or use criticism. Compliment him when he finally brushes his teeth: "Wow, I'm blinded by the shine coming off the whiteness of your teeth!"

Granted, this approach only works with a child who is higher functioning and has the ability to do self-care. For those individuals who have lower functioning abilities, they will require a caregiver to give daily assistance for their hygiene and other self-care.

Repetitive behaviors accompany daily living for those with autism. Behaviors such as, pacing, hand flapping, tip toe walking and repeating words or sounds. "Repetitive phrases" doesn't clearly describe the frequency with which our boys ramble off lines from the latest movie they've seen or a phrase from a song they have heard. They also have frequent audible conversations with themselves.

There are also times when they just won't sit still or stay in a designated space. Our boys are frequently bouncing up and down or pacing all around the house. We usually apply brain exercises to help minimize their noises and restless behaviors. However, other tools can be used for the instances when we are in a place where it wouldn't work to apply these techniques.

I recently heard a couple of ideas from a behavioral specialist, Terri Drca, that I think are ingenious for helping with situations when a child's behavior appears awkward. For the talkative child, get her a non-working cell phone or blue tooth that she can talk into and nobody will know that she is talking to herself. For the child who is restless and moves around a lot, give him earphones to wear, even if he doesn't have an iPod or MP3 player to plug the ear phones into so others can think they are dancing to music. (Of course I think it would be more enjoyable for your child to have music actually playing.)

> *I wish I had one or two hours*
> *to pick his brain so I could find out*
> *what I need to do to help him.*
>
> *– Kiersten*

There isn't a cure for autism, but there is still hope. There are many treatment methods available, and most actually help. However, be careful of those that offer a "cure" but fail to bring the promised results. Educate yourself on treatment options. Find out what the benefits are, who has tried it, and what the results were. Ask questions: Will this treatment option have any side effects? What are the costs?

Unfortunately, some of the better treatment options are expensive. Trust your instincts as a parent and go with what you feel is best after you have done the research. *What works for one might not work for another.* It's likely that your child will need multiple methods of treatment, because each method is addressing a different challenge. See if the treatment meets the goals to improve your child's brain function, developmental abilities, and her quality of life.

Allow time to see the results from a treatment method. Give it a month. If it works, continue with the program. Try only one new method at a time so you can identify what is working. Also know that certain treatments may help for a time, but later may need to be adjusted as new challenges surface.

> *Autism is caused by a difference*
> *in the hardwiring of the brain.*
> *This is an important concept*
> *for others to understand,*
> *because it indicates that*
> *there is no medicine or drug*
> *that can cure autism.*
>
> *– Cliff*

Medication

Medication is a sensitive topic. Making a decision to medicate is a matter of personal choice for the child's parents to decide. **There isn't a magic pill to make your child's challenges go away or make her brain function properly. Some medications can help manage and relieve some of the behaviors and medical conditions that need addressing.** Medications should only be administered under a doctor's supervision.

Before your child begins taking any drug your physician recommends, research it. Talk to a pharmacist about side effects. Find out what the benefits are. After your child begins the medication, make careful observations to see if it improves the symptoms or makes the issues worse.

I am glad we waited to use medication for a couple of our sons. We wanted to see the benefits from natural methods of treatments before introducing a drug. Some medications made one son's symptoms worse. When we did try medications, one drug resulted in more insomnia and weight loss; another son had exaggerated repetitive behaviors; and one type of medication brought on behaviors we had never seen before. It took some time to find something that helped address some of our sons' challenges. Not all of our boys take medication, and we hope the ones who do, don't become dependent on it.

If you notice negative side effects and you don't feel your child should continue taking the medication, talk to your doctor about having him discontinue use. Stopping a medication abruptly may result in negative or life – threatening side effects.

Diet

Autism is often linked with digestion issues. If a child has poor eating habits, sensitivities to food, or digestive issues, a special diet is commonly recommended. Many parents, have tried or use the gluten- free, casein-free (GFCF) diet. Some give herbal supplements, try natural remedies, or other expensive diets to treat autistic symptoms. **Diet changes have helped a small percentage of children make remarkable improvements.** However, the products are not guaranteed to work with everyone. For the small percentage that do benefit, it is a wonderful relief and blessing.

A good diet is important for everyone's health.
Eliminating foods that are unhealthy and increasing those that are healthy would improve the health of all individuals whether or not they have autism. Watch for certain foods that aggravate the individual's symptoms and make challenges more difficult. Consider taking to a physician or nutritional specialist. Again, do some research and look at all the possibilities before jumping into what seems to promise results, and then determine your best option.

Chapter 4

Special Education Services

I wish others appreciated
children with autism for who they are.
They have so much to offer us
if we give them a chance.
They have many more
abilities than disabilities.

– Carol

Every child with a learning disability in the United States is entitled to a special education that will accommodate his or her needs. Most schools aren't standing at the door waiting to give that help, however. The process is very long and entails large amounts of paperwork, meetings, and testing as you set individual goals for your child.

Learning disabilities often accompany autistic challenges. This is usually a result of the child's developmental delays. You can have your child evaluated at school by the school psychologist, but it takes a very long time. They have 45 days to conduct their tests and evaluations. Some schools will accept a clinical diagnosis, but they will conduct their own evaluation of the child before beginning services. Expect it to take a long time before special education services start.

For those who have a need that is impeding their education schools are required to provide special education services within the least restrictive environment. The special education committee will decide what "least restrictive environment" is best for your child's education. This committee is comprised of the child's teacher, school administrators, special education teachers, the school psychologist, and at times a speech therapist, occupational therapist, or district representative, and most importantly at least one parent.

Classroom placement is determined by the child's needs. The child's placement can change depending on what is in her best interest—which is determined by her improvements, regressions, or other circumstances. A diagnosis of a disorder or disability does not guarantee your child will receive special education services. In order to receive services, her history and evaluation needs to show that her disability affects her learning or academic abilities. A child can have autism and not qualify for special education services if the disability does not impede her education at school or home.

I love early intervention.
It has taught me so much, and
I have seen such an improvement
over the last six months with my son!
It saved my family!

– Kiersten

Early Intervention

Early intervention services are for children under three years of age. If a child shows significant developmental delays or has a diagnosis of autism, he or she is eligible for early intervention services through the school district. The child will receive an individualized family service plan (IFSP). Specialists will come to the home to help address the child's needs and train the parents on how to implement therapies at home.

Individual Education Program

When a child is old enough for preschool, he is evaluated to determine what services he will need in school. **If he meets the requirements, he will have an individual education program (IEP). The IEP document is for all persons working with the child on his educational goals—parents, teachers, special education teachers, and the psychologist.**

If your child doesn't receive an IEP, you can try to get him a 504 plan, which will still help provide some services. A 504 plan insures the rights of each individual with disabilities to be included in receiving an education and to have modifications and accommodations provided so that the individual has the opportunity to perform at the same level as his peers.

In the IEP, goals are set for the following 12 months or for a school year. The IEP team works on improving the child's academic goals. A behavior plan may be implemented that addresses other needs at school. The special education committee sets the goals for the child. Services that may be provided include one to three hours outside of his regular classroom each day to help him learn the basics: math, reading, and writing. Or he may be placed in a class that has a smaller teacher-to-student ratio, to accommodate his needs.

Each year, the IEP team meets together to discuss the child's progress and if any changes need to be made to the IEP. The child is also re-evaluated for services every three years. As a parent you have the right to request additional meetings to change the IEP and to discuss the progress of your child. You may request a rough draft of the IEP to review before the meeting in order to have a better understanding of what to expect or to note any changes you want to make.

It is important to keep a hard copy of each IEP document and any other documents related to your child on file at home. Doing so will save you time and energy. Many situations will arise when you will need these documents, even after your child becomes an adult.

As you prepare for your child's transition to adulthood, have a local vocational rehabilitation representative come to the IEP meetings when your child is 14 years old and older. Have questions ready to ask such as "What is available for him when he is able to start working?" Explain your child's struggles; perhaps he has difficulty interviewing, arriving on time, or keeping the job especially after having a meltdown or getting upset.

I wish teachers would challenge
my child's strengths and
be understanding of his weaknesses.

– Fiona

Educators, watch this video: *Essentials for Educators: High Functioning Autism Asperger Syndrome*. This video is also excellent for other teachers or leaders (such as church teachers, and scout leaders). It gives great ideas for the classroom. Here, educators share their personal and professional experiences on how include and incorporate these children into the classroom and how to help them learn. You can find the video on YouTube or on the Website for the Autism Council of Utah: http://autismcouncilofutah.org/life-with-autism/best-practices/

To you who have a trained eye for detecting autistic symptoms: Find a way to share what you have noticed with the parents without showing judgment or placing blame.

In social settings, I have a
Spock-like range of emotional display.
When you listen to me,
There is little emotion in my voice,
so it may be difficult to "read" me.
My voice may be as confusing as text.

– Fiona

Social Skills

Most of us naturally internalize social skills by watching others around us. Temple Grandin talks about social skills training in her book, *Thinking in Pictures*. She says, **"Teaching a person with autism social graces is like coaching an actor for a play. Every**

step has to be planned" (Grandin, 101). It is difficult for those with autism to read facial expressions and to pick up on social cues. Their autistic thought process is very different when they are interacting with others. Therefore, social skills training is important in helping them learn how to "read" others and respond appropriately.

Some interactive social skills programs are available that can make learning them fun. You can find programs online, in books, and on DVDs, some can be found in local libraries. Few schools incorporate social skills training. *The Unwritten Rules of Social Relationships,* by Temple Grandin and Sean Barron explain how to teach individuals with autism what social skills and manners are appropriate.

You can ask a well-trained teacher or professional for help as well. They know how to teach children how to act and what to say in social settings.

Occupational and Physical Therapy

Occupational therapy (OT) and physical therapy (PT) are used to help improve fine-and-gross motor skills and to help individuals with their sensory challenges. OT and PT therapy may address life skills, including walking and eating.

Our oldest son had to learn fine-motor skills—such as how to grasp a pencil correctly in order to write. Although he improved enough to write his letters and words, he still struggles with penmanship. He also had lessons in using scissors. It was a hidden blessing that as a young boy he wasn't cutting things he shouldn't, but he still needed to learn how to use them.

Speech Therapy

Speech therapy is a service received by most children with autism because of their communication delays. Speech therapy is included in school services for the child that has communication delays. The frequency of speech therapy services is determined by the level of the child's delay. It took a few years and several dedicated speech therapists before our oldest son was using full sentences—a skill he obtained when he was five.

Technological devices such as computers and iPads are being developed and aid those with special needs. They are being incorporated into schools. These technological devices are unlocking nonverbal imprisonment for those who struggle to communicate. As individuals learn to type on a keyboard or tap on a flat screen, they are able to communicate their thoughts, emotions, and needs.

Autism has MANY faces;
some people with autism can be successful
in many areas of their lives and have only
one or two areas that are challenging.

– Linda

Services are not guaranteed for adults with autism. Nor do these adults have the entitlements they once had when they attended primary and secondary schools. Their special education services continue until they are 22 years old. After that, they will have to meet eligibility requirements for services, and those services are usually only for those who have the most severe challenges. If they are not able to care for themselves as adults, their parents will need to apply for guardianship. Also, it is wise to apply for supplemental security income (SSI) and Medicaid when they are18. This will help provide financial assistance for medical needs and the costs of daily living.

The Division of Services for People with Disabilities (DSPD) provides assistance to the caregiver and the child. Apply as soon as you can; preferably when the child is young. It may be years or, for some, decades before the individual receives services. In most states there is a long waiting list. Where your child is placed on that list is determined by several factors—the severity of the disability, the life circumstances of the family (including the financial ability and health of the parents), and the availability of a good support network (church, extended family or community supports). If any of these factors change so would the your child's placement on that list, services could be given sooner or later. Those whose needs are severe or whose living conditions or family circumstances are limited receive services first.

When children turn 12 years old, the law affecting them changes. Your child's innocence and lack of ability to read social cues may result in others making incorrect assumptions and misunderstanding his behavior. His activity may be seen as suspicious or against the law.

As a child or as an adult, there are also concerns for his safety. Adults with autism are *not* as aware of danger as people who are neuro-typical, and they often do not have a true sense of fear. They may run out into the street, run off and not know their way back, be accident prone, impulsive, or ingest toxic substances. They may be naive to manipulation by those pretending to befriend them with the intent to exploit or abuse them. Set up a secure home and surrounding environment. Inform trusted neighbors of the possible dangers so they can help look out for your child's well being.

> *Courage is being scared to death –*
> *but saddling up anyway.*
>
> *– John Wayne*
> *(Brainy Quote)*

Who Needs to Know that He Has Autism?

Those who have frequent interaction with him, such as a teacher, therapist, family member, friend, or neighbor. These are those who need the information. You don't have to tell strangers you meet at the store or other parents at school. Not everyone has to know he has autism. Would you introduce yourself saying, *"Hello my name is . . . and I have a fear of spiders and need to wear glasses when I read."*

How to Tell Others?

When telling those who need to know, find or schedule an opportunity to talk about what autism is and how it affects your child. You could offer them an informative book or have them visit a reputable resource or Website. Be sure to tell those who are closest to you and your child, so they have a better understanding of what to do in difficult situations. More than likely they want to help; they just don't know how. Educating those closest to you helps them understand your struggles and also helps them recognize the amazing things your child can do, despite his functional ability.

Talk to your child about her challenges. Teach her when to disclose information to others so it doesn't cause embarrassment to her or to the person receiving the information. Teach her child how to talk about her disability in a way that will help a teacher, friend, or employer know what help she will need.

People with autism CAN learn
all the concepts a neuro-typical person can learn —
it just takes much,
much more practice and repetition.

– Cliff

Chapter 5

How to Be Supportive

*It's hard to describe someone who can be
an angel in one situation and a devil in another.
She simply does not have the same thought
processes that "normal" people have
and so in some situations she doesn't act
like "normal" people would.*

– Linda

**Watch *Autism Every Day* on the Website
AutismSpeaks.org or on YouTube.com.** This will give you a
glimpse of the struggles those with moderate to severe autism face. If
you want to know what life is like for a family that deals with a
family member with autism, go spend a day or two with them. It's
true: Seeing is believing. The following are some wonderful insights
from those who know.

How Can I Show Support?

**Awareness and understanding is the key to showing
support.** Most parents feel that loved ones, who don't spend
enough time with their child have a tendency to minimize the
families struggles and the child's challenges. It is embarrassing to
hear complete strangers say rude or hurtful comments to those
with autism or to their parents. It's even worse to hear insensitive
or cruel words from a family member or a friend. Here are some
of the insensitive comments or criticisms I've received: "Your
child doesn't look autistic." "I don't want my child to play with

him." "It's just a phase. He will grow out of it." "If only you would discipline him more, he would behave better."

If you have made a comment to someone that may have hurt, ask for forgiveness. **What you are seeing is likely mild compared to the struggles the child and his family encounter every day.**

Here is a list of some don'ts:

- **Don't judge. Most parents are doing *EVERYTHING* they know how to do.** Understand that each individual's challenges are unique and different from yours; so don't assume you know all the answers.
- **Don't** assume you know what it is like to have a child with autism.
- **Don't** talk to someone with autism as though she is stupid or as if she is not there. You may be amazed at how much she understands despite her limited abilities.
- **Don't** exclude the child from activities. She will know, and it will hurt—even if she doesn't appear to notice.
- **Don't** give the impression that you think the parents are inadequate, express doubt or deny that the child has an ASD. Your doubt shows a lack of support and squashes the parents' efforts and thus can hinder that child's progress. If there is a misdiagnosis, then let a second professional do the evaluating.
- **Don't** give advice unless advice is requested by the parent or child.

- **Don't** say, "Let me know if I can help." Instead ask, "How can I help?" and then offer something specific you can do!

*I wish I had had more support from my family
at the beginning instead of having them think
I was crazy or being too paranoid.
I knew something was wrong,
and no one would listen.*

– Kiersten

I have talked to many parents of children with autism. Nearly every parent has said to me, ***"I wish others would believe me and have a clear understanding of what it is like to parent a child with autism."*** Parents have also told me how embarrassing it is to have gawkers stare at their child or at their family as if they are fish in a fish bowl. When their child is having a meltdown or blowup, *they don't want an audience*. Their family crisis is not a spectator sport or an audition for a play.

When someone's child is having an emotional episode, many people wonder how to respond. Well-meaning family and friends want to offer assistance, but usually (and unintentionally) get in the way. The natural first response is to reach out to help and to move closer to the child. However, this triggers the fight or flight response in the child and merely escalates the situation.

Here are some things you can do in instead:

Give the parent and child some space—a quiet, private place where the parent can take her child and help him to calm down. It is in the best interest of all involved to remove the child from the situation or to ask others to clear the room. More than likely the trigger for the child's episode came from the environment they are in or from the difficulties of a transition.

You can offer to help with things that don't directly affect the interaction between the parent and the child who is struggling. For instance, you can offer to carry something for the parent; you can offer to help gather up their things (when the parent is trying to leave); or you can offer to care for their other child or children. Remember, the dads can use help, too!

Parents love their children and are doing their best. **Tell the parents you have confidence in their abilities.** Your faith in them will empower them, and this will help them to help their child. They are the ones giving the greatest amounts of time and effort to assist in their child's development and growth.

Here's some more "Do's" that may help:

- **Be** a support for the parents, especially the one who is the primary caregiver (usually the mom). She is giving the majority of the care and expending all of her time and energy for her special-needs child. (Typical mothering times 100!)

- **Do** give the parents your respect and confidence. They are amazing. Let them know they are doing a great job, and tell them what you admire about them.
- **Help** with chores and errands.
- **Offer** to bring in or order dinner.
- **Offer** to babysit or pay for a qualified respite provider so the mom and dad can have a night out
- **Listen** with an open heart and mind. Mom or Dad might just need someone to talk to.
- **Believe** the parents.
- **Be** understanding.
- **Give** the parent a hug.
- **Talk** to the individual with autism like you would any other child. He can understand more than you realize.
- **Find out** what therapy tool or toy the child needs or likes and give that to her for Christmas, a birthday, or just because.
- **Be willing** to educate yourself about autism spectrum disorders. Learn about the child's specific autistic challenges. Ask questions. If you feel like your question is dumb or could be insulting, preface it by saying, "I am unaware of what autism is really like. Could I ask you a question? "

- If a parent refuses an offer family and friends might think they can't help. Offering help lets the parents know that you care. Honestly, most parents wish they could accept the offer, another time might be better. Don't stop offering and giving help.

Kiersten shares her appreciation for the support she receives: "I love my support system of family and friends. It's so nice to be able to rejoice in my child's successes with someone who really understands. It helps to be able to cry on a shoulder because my son hasn't made a new step in weeks! I love having friends and family to call when he has finally made a big step, and I just need to shout it out!"

Mom tends to neglect herself
as a result of all the sacrifices
she makes for her children.
SHE NEEDS A BREAK!
Give her enough time to take care of herself
and get recharged to face
the next day's challenges.
If you can help give her that needed break,
you are heaven-sent.

Befriending Someone with Autism

You can be the friend of someone with autism even if he avoids you, invades your personal space, or has some other unique behavior. Talk to him. Sit by him. Find out what interests him and use those interests as an avenue to connect with him. If he isolates himself or appears rude or awkward, love him anyway, and ask the parents what you can do to show that you care.

Once you know the child and understand his interests and needs—and if the parents approve, you can go for a walk with him to help him lower his anxieties. Following the guidance of the parents, help him learn to desensitize from over stimuli or help him calm down after an emotional episode.

Anna, a mom of a preschooler with autism, shares her desires to have her son included: "As a mom with a preschooler and toddler on the autism spectrum, I often feel lonely. We aren't asked to have play dates. Parents and kids don't know how to "play" with my child. We are usually excluded not only from play dates, but also from home school, preschools, parties, and other group outings. Sometimes others are right in assuming that the activity wouldn't be a good fit for my child, but it is always nice to be asked anyway. If a parent does not accept an invitation (or even 25 invitations), please don't stop inviting or trying to include them. Sometimes merely your desire to include is the best support you can offer."

Church and Community Involvement

Educate the leaders, the congregation or group about autism. Many families stop attending functions because they feel judged, embarrassed, or because it is so difficult to managing their children in difficult environments. Families who have a child with autism will feel more comfortable at church and in the community if those they interact with understand.

Find ways to include individuals with autism. Set up accommodations so they can participate as much as possible and

NEVER exclude them. It may be difficult at first to incorporate these accommodations.

Ask leaders to assign a teacher or helper to work specifically with the individual with autism. Offer to train the teacher or helper as well.

Designate a safe place for the times when the child needs to calm down. Establish a pattern or schedule so the child will be comfortable. Once patterns or schedules are set, all may benefit.

Laura helps us better understanding the choices parents make when they are in difficult situations. She says, "Don't be offended if the family has to leave an activity or event or even takes off mid-sentence without an explanation. They have probably reached their max, and it is in the best interest for all involved to be able to leave. This helps stop the behavior from continuing or possibly escalating to a situation beyond their control."

Communicate Effectively

For the most part, **talk in your normal voice** to the child with autism; do not use a "baby voice."

Make eye contact, even if he doesn't look back. Even if you notice a child isn't responding with eye contact or words, she is still listening to you. To exchange eye contact with my sons, I usually only answer their questions when they look at me.

Teach in a literal sense, give black and white instructions, and set up clear rules and structure. Avoid sarcasm, puns, and idioms. Most individuals will take your words literally. A child with autism will look for animals coming from the sky when you say, "It's raining cats and dogs," or will wonder where the cake is when you say, "It's a piece of cake." Beware of saying "Bite me," or you might get teeth marks on your skin.

Talk low, talk slow, and don't say too much

– John Wayne
(Brainy Quote)

Learn how that child communicates. Ask the parents if they are using sign language, gestures, or a picture exchange communication system (PECS) to increase their child's ability to communicate.

Below is an explanation from my friend Fiona who is on the autism spectrum. She describes her frustration as an adult with her communication and social interactions. This may give you insight in how to interact with others who have autism as well.

She says, "Sometimes I can't think of anything to say. People think I'm ignoring them, but my wheels are spinning, and I just can't come up with an answer or an appropriate response. I get so stuck with those smoking thinking wheels that I forget to even say, 'Let me think about that,' or 'I'm not sure.' It's even more difficult when you add to the equation the social dynamics of a large group who are chit-chatting. It is hard to know when I would be interrupting verses contributing. It is hard to find conversational material that would be appreciated by the entire audience. I will either freeze up or say 'to heck with it' and just say what I want when I want. Either way, socializing with a group is tricky business!

"Sometimes I know if I speak, I will offend," She continues. "So I stay quiet, because I consider the other person's feelings, even when SOMETHING should be said. I don't want to say anything about some of the things they're doing that makes me uncomfortable, so I just quietly leave. And then I get in trouble because I am 'avoiding them and not considering their feelings.' No, I'm just a bad guesser. And I didn't know I needed to excuse myself when we hadn't really been talking or doing anything together at the time I left. There are just too many unwritten rules for me to remember.

"I HATE asking for help, because I am so uncomfortable making others uncomfortable. If I have to make a phone call to get help, that's a double discomfort. Sometimes I say something benign, and people, to my surprise and detriment, put a grouchy twist on it. I hate the phone.

"For those of us with Aspergers, we have a VERY hard time imagining other people's thoughts or understanding their actions. It is so much easier to just have the other person say, 'What you said hurt my feelings.' Instead most will give a subtle comment that I cannot interperte and that leaves me bewildered. It's worse when out of the blue, (from my perspective) a person starts 'spewing poison' into what I thought was a perfectly calm discussion.

"PLEASE don't 'drop hints' to people with Asperger Syndrome! We need straightforward communication. We need things spelled out. No, it isn't obvious to us. No one can read minds, but many neuro-typical people are pretty good at guessing, but those with Asperger's are not.

"There are so many variables to social interaction and communication. Asperger folks are trying to figure out how people react by trying to put other's behaviors into a complex formulae. For instance my thought process when I'm talking to someone might be; since she said <u>this</u>, then she feels <u>that</u> way. But she only feels that way if certain conditions are in place. However, those assumptions may not apply when she is sick or too tired.

"What it adds up to is that we are bad at guessing what others are thinking and feeling, and if we do guess, we guess wrong. We aren't trying to offend. But if we do offend you, PLEASE explain how we did, so we won't do it again."

I hope this book has raised your awareness and given you better understanding. If you are interested, I encourage you to learn more. Most importantly, I hope you will be a support to the adult or child that has an ASD and to his or her family. You can increase awareness and understanding in those you know.

If you are a parent of a child with ASD, create a team of individuals to give you support and aid you in your efforts.

My husband and I are still learning how to parent our sons. We continue to make improvements and learn from others and from our own experiences in both good and bad.

My boys are my heroes. They demonstrate strength and courage—a hero's courage—to overcome the obstacles and challenges they face each day.

A hero is an ordinary individual
who finds the strength
to persevere and endure
in spite of overwhelming obstacle

– Christopher Reeves
(Brainy Quote)

Additional Information and Resources

Online

Autism Speaks. Website: autismspeaks.org. This site is a great resource. Here, you'll find news and events, statistics, tool kits, and ways to connect to other parents

Autism Counsel of Utah. Website: autismcouncilofutah.org. The Autism Counsel organizes events and works to raise awareness about autism. The following link is to a video about how to help those with autism in school. It is also helpful for community activity leaders. http://autismcouncilofutah.org/life-with-autism/best-practices/

First Signs. Website: firstsigns.org. Here you learn the first signs of autism so you can recognize them in your child.

Utah Parent Center. Website: www.utahparentcenter.org. Phone: (801) 272-1051. The Utah Parent Center provides resource lists, referrals, training, and information on autism.

DSM Diagnostic Criteria. Web page: http://www.firstsigns.org/screening/DSM4.htm. On this page you will find a copy of the *Diagnostics Statistical Manuel of Mental Disorders* (DSM) IV edition, Sections 299.00, 299.10, 299.80.

DSM V Proposals – This Website: American Psychiatric Association site is where you can find the current proposed changes for the *Diagnostic Statistical Manual of Mental Health* for the fifth edition. http://www.dsm5.org

Support

Allies With Families. (801) 433-2595. Provides support and resources for parents and children who face serious emotional, behavioral, and mental health challenges.

Autism: Understanding the Puzzle. You can find helpful information, links to resources, and practical experience at autismunderstandingthepuzzle.blogspot.com. or e-mail your questions to me at understandingthepuzzle@hotmail.com.

"Big MAK's" (Mothers of Autistic Kids) utahmaks.blogspot.com. This group of mothers meets monthly for lunch; locations change each month. On this blog you can find the lunch location and other helpful information about other events, support, and contacts to additional resources.

David School District Parent Consultant, Roz Welch (801) 402-5120, rozw@utahparentcenter.org. She will answer your questions about special education in school, Individual Education Program (IEP)'s, and your rights and responsibilities under the Individuals with Disabilities Education Act (IDEA).

F.A.A.S.T (Families of Autism and Asperger's Standing Together). Is about helping families have an avenue for support and to spread the awareness for Autism and Asperger's. You can find them on Facebook and at this website http://faastutah.weebly.com

Mental Health in Utah, "On The Edge". Do you want to know more about Mental Health in Utah? If you have an hour to watch this very informative video, "On The Edge: Mental Health in Utah" it will give you a better understanding to what is really happening and what you can do to help.

http://www.kued.org/ontheedge/?area=watch-online

PAAS (Parents Autism Awareness Support). They are on Facebook and work to help spread autism awareness and offer support for families.

Support Group through Wee Care Pediatrics. Contact Kandise Wilde, kwilde@wcpeds.com to sign up. Your child does not need to be a patient at Wee Care Pediatrics to attend the parent support group. The group is available to anyone dealing with the challenges of autism.

Utah Parent Center. Parents helping parents of children with disabilities. http://www.utahparentcenter.org/

<u>Diagnostics</u>

University of Utah Behavioral Health Clinic
650 Komas Dr. #208, Salt Lake City, UT 84108
(801) 585-1212

Autism Assessment and Treatment Center
www.autismutah.com
4505 Wasatch Blvd. Suite 190, Salt Lake City, UT 84124
(801) 386-8069

The Children's Center
http://www.tccslc.org/
350 South 400 East, Salt Lake City, UT 84111
(801)-582-5534

Pediatricians

Check your insurance for a pediatrician that specializes in autistic patients with autism. Here are two physicians that I know are good.

Dr. Lisa Palmieri
9500 South 1300 East Sandy, UT 84094,
(801) 501-2100

Dr. Catherine Strasser
2075 North 1200 West, Layton, UT 84041,
(801) 779-6200

Therapy

Attachment Therapy. Website: www.attachment.org. Here, you will find therapists who work with parents and children on emotional and behavioral challenges.

Horse Therapy. Website: www.hoofbeats.us. Contact Tami Tanner at (801) 836-4325 or tami@hoofbeats.us. Tami works with special-needs clients who have disabilities such as autism, Down syndrome, and trauma disorders.

Sensory Integration. Primary Children's Pediatric Rehabilitation Center provides occupational therapy (OT) and physical therapy (PT) services. There are seven offices in Utah. These are two that I've used: Bountiful (801) 292-8665 and Ogden (801) 387-2080.

Respite Care

Division of Services for People with Disabilities (DSPD)
195 North 1950 West, Salt Lake City, UT 84116
(801) 538-4200 or 1-800-837-6811
www.dspd.utah.gov

CTA Community Support Center
4444 South 700 East Suite 203
Murray, UT 84107
(801) 268-4887
http://ctautah.org/

Family Support Center (two locations)
2020 South Lake St., Salt Lake City, UT 84105
(801) 487-7778

777 W. Center Street (7720 South), Midvale, UT 84047
(801) 255-6881
www.familysupportcenter.org/nursery

Schools

Go to your local school district's website and look for contact information for the special needs department, and they will direct you to evaluation and services needed for your child. Here are a few contacts we have worked with in Utah.

Davis School District. Website: www.davis.k12.ut.us.
(801) 402-5169.

Jordan School District. Website: www.jordandistrict.org.
(801) 567-8176.

For additional school district contact information, look at
Utah Education Network www.uen.org/Districts/k12.cgi
and click on District Offices.

Carmen B. Pingree. Private school for children and teens with autism.
Website: www.carmenbpingree.com.
780 S Guardsman Way, Salt Lake City, UT 84018
(801) 581-0194

Spectrum Academy. *Charter school.* Website: www.spectrumcharter.org.
Elementary (801) 936-0318, select 1
575 North Cutler Dr., North Salt Lake, UT 84054
Junior High and High School (801) 936-0318, select 2
665 North Cutler Dr., North Salt Lake, UT 84054

Books and Good Reads

Elder, Jennifer. ***Different Like Me.*** London and Philadelphia: Jessica
Kingsley Publishers, 2006.

Grandin, Temple. ***Thinking In Pictures: and Other Reports from My Life
with Autism.*** New York: Vintage Books, 1995.

Grandin, Temple and Sean Barron. ***The Unwritten Rules Of Social
Relationships.*** Arlington: Future Horizons, 2005.

Grandin, Temple. ***The Way I See it: A Personal Look at Autism and
Aspergers.*** Arlington: Future Horizons, 2008.

Hoopman, Kathy. ***All Cats Have Aspergers Syndrome.*** London and
Philadelphia: Jessica Kingsley Publishers, 2006.

Jackson, Luke. ***Freaks, Geeks and Asperger's Syndrome: A User Guide to
Adolescence.*** London and Philadelphia: Jessica Kingsley Publishers, 2002.

Kranowitz, Carol Stock and Lucy Jane Miller. ***The Out-of-Sync Child:
Recognizing and Coping with Sensory Processing Disorder.*** Revised
edition. New York: Berkley Publishing Group, 2005.

Kranowitz, Carol Stock. *The Out-of-Sync Child Has Fun: Activities for Kids with Sensory Processing Disorder*. Revised edition. New York: Penguin Group, 2003.

Notbohm, Ellen. *Ten Things Every Child with Autism Wishes You Knew*. Arlington: Future Horizons, Inc., 2005.

Welton, Jude. *Can I Tell You About Asperger Syndrome?: A Guide for Friends and Family*. London and New York: Jessica Kingsley Publishers, 2004.

Wrobel, Mary. *Taking Care of Myself: A Hygiene, Puberty and Personal Curriculum for Young People with Autism.* Arlington: Future Horizons, Inc., 2003.

Kingsley, Emily Perl. **"Welcome to Holland."** 1987. <http://www.creativeparents.com/Holland.html.>

Movies and TV

Temple Grandin. Director Mick Jackson. Actress Claire Danes. HBO films. February 2010. A movie about the life story of Dr. Temple Grandin and how she overcame her challenges and used her strengths to be successful in life.

Wretches and Jabbers. Director Gerardine Wurzburg. Actors Larry Bissonnette and Tracy Thresher. John P. Huntsman Foundation and the Autism Society. April 2011. A movie documenting the story of two men—Larry and Tracy—along with a few of their friends who are nonverbal, and how they communicate through technological devices. Currently is only in selected theaters.

Monk. Creator: Andy Breckman. Actors Tony Shalhoub, Jason Gray-Stanford and Ted Levine. USA Network. July 2002. A comedic television series about an obsessive compulsive detective, Adrian Monk, a detective who has obsessive compulsive disorder. He helps solve crimes in San Francisco using his amazing attention to detail, while also dealing the challenges of Asperger syndrome.

Bibliography

American Psychiatric Association. *Diagnostic and Statistical Manual of Mental Disorders,* 4th Edition. Sections 299.00, 299.10, 299.80. Washington D.C.: American Psychiatric Association, 2000.

—."Proposed Revisions to DSM Disorders and Criteria." Section *A 09 Autism Spectrum Disorder.* Diagnostic and Statistical Manual of Mental Disorders, 5th Edition. *American Psychiatric Association.* Revised January 26, 2011. Accessed August 2011 <http://www.dsm5.org/ProposedRevisions/Pages/Proposedrevision.aspx?rid=94#>.

Autism Speaks. "100 Day Kit." *Autism Speaks.* 2005-2011. Accessed August 2011 <http://www.autismspeaks.org/family-services/tool-kits/100-day-kit>.

—. "Learn the Signs of Autism." *Autism Speaks.* 2005-2011. Accessed August 2011 <http://www.autismspeaks.org/what-autism/learn-signs>.

—. "What is Autism?" *Autism Speaks.* 2005-2011. Accessed August 2011 <http://www.autismspeaks.org/what-autism>.

Belnap, W. Dean. "A Brain Gone Wrong": How the Brain/Body Reacts to Anxiety and Stress. *Meridian Magazine.* August 9, 2006. Accessed September 2011. http://www.freerepublic.com/focus/f-chat/168023/posts.

Brainy Quote. "Christopher Reeve Quotes." *BookRags Media Network.* 2001-2011. Accessed August 2011 < http://brainyquote.com/quotes/quotes/c/christophe141891.html>.

—. "Will Rogers Quotes." *BookRags Media Network.* 2001-2011. Accessed August 2011 <http://www.brainyquote.com/quotes/quotes/w/willrogers104938.html>.

—. "John Wayne Quotes." *BookRags Media Network.* 2001-2011. Accessed August 2011 <http://www.brainyquote.com/quotes/quotes/j/johnwayne100060.html>.

Centers for Disease Control and Prevention: Autism and Developmental Disabilities Monitoring Network. "Autism Spectrum Disorders." *Centers For Disease Control and Prevention.* July 26, 2011. Accessed August 2011 <http://www.cdc.gov/ncbddd/autism/addm.html>.

Fitzgerald, Michael and O'Brien, Brendan. *Genius Genes How Asperger Talents Changed the World.* Kansas: Autism Asperger Publishing Company, 2007.

Grandin, Temple. *Thinking In Pictures: and Other Reports from My Life with Autism.* New York: Vintage Books, 1995.

Leonard, Wendy. "Utah autism rate doubled between '02-'08 data shows." *KSL.com.* May 6, 2011. Accessed August 2011 <http://www.ksl.com/?nid=960&sid=15440761&s_cid=rss-960>.

Mayo Clinic Staff. "Childhood Disintegrative Disorder." *Mayo Clinic.* September 16, 2010. Accessed March 2011. <http://www.mayoclinic.com/health/childhood-disintegrative-disorder/DS00801/DSECTION=symptoms>.

—. "Rett's Syndrome." *Mayo Clinic.* July 18, 2010. Accessed March 2011 <http://www.mayoclinic.com/health/rett-syndrome/DS00716>.

National Institue of Mental Health. "Autism Spectrum Disorders (Pervasive Developmental Disorders)." *NIMH.* December 8, 2010. Accessed August 2011 <http://www.nimh.nih.gov/health/publications/autism/complete-index.shtml>.

Tanner, Lindsey. "Autism risk for siblings are higher than thought." *KSL.com.* August 15, 2011. Accessed August 2011 <http://www.ksl.com/?nid=201&sid=16811300>.

"What is Rett Syndrome?" Rett Syndrome Research Trust. 2008. Accessed August 2011 <http://rsrt.org/about-Rett/>.

YMCA of USA, Dartmouth Medical School, and Institute for American Values. "Hardwired to Connect: The New Scientific Case for Authoritative Community." Stephen J Bavolek, ed. *Nurturing Parenting.com.* 2007. Accessed May 2011 <http://www.nurturingparenting.com/research_validation/hardwire d_to_connect.pdf >.